I Am From

Voices from a Prison in the South

Imprint Universal Consciousness Publications

Published in 2020 by
Nuvo Development, Inc.
Decatur, GA 30034

No one can change more completely
than the man who has been at the bottom.

Malcolm X

We realize the importance of our own voices
only when we are silenced.

Malala Yousafzai

Contributors

Introduction

Voice is a powerful agent of change. Whether they are the voices of those left behind in slave narratives, the autobiographies, and biographies of freedom fighters, like Harriet Tubman, Frederick Douglas, or Malcolm X, or whether they are those of men living in a homeless shelter, that I interviewed myself, I have always been interested in the voices of the downtrodden and oppressed. And this is because of how their voices have not only moved me but how they have empowered and inspired me.

Whether their situation was due to circumstances beyond their control, e.g. their birth or injustices, particularly those that set in motion circumstances that lead to criminalization, or whether it was due to their own makings, what I have found particularly inspiring is how they were able to turn their circumstances into triumphs. But more importantly, it is how using their voices serve to transform and empower others.

Not only do voices of the past inspire and empower future generations, but they also etch in time what life was like when they lived. When one finds their voices, they will discover that there is no distance between us and those who left them behind. For words that seek to lift and inspire, there is no time, only transcendence.

I have always been interested in the voices of men who have found themselves in the unfortunate situation of being incarcerated in an American prison. I have been curious about what their lives were like before becoming incarcerated, what led to their incarceration, their experiences in prison, what it has and is teaching them, lessons learned, and where they are in terms of their perspectives and outlook. Although the poems in *I am From* come nowhere near to accomplishing all of this, they still give us some insights into the early experiences and perspectives of some of the contributors and they serve to inspire those who read them.

When I reached out to David about my interest in co-editing an anthology of writings from men in prison, surprisingly, he indicated that he was a facilitator and mentor in a program that many offenders volunteer to participate in for the purpose of improving their lives by obtaining information through erudition and attending courses offered by the institution. In one particular course, facilitated by Hugo Lacasidon and others, the men were required to write a poem in which each sentence begins with: "I Am From," and include references to food, places, language, family, religion, etc.

When I received the first set of *I am From* poems, words cannot describe how moved I was by some of them, and that experience continued with each new set, some moving me to tears. *I Am From* tells us who these men were before they became incarcerated and gives us a glimpse into who some of them are now.

From what I was able to extract from their poems, the men are a diverse population. Some of them are from other countries; Mexico, El Salvador, Israel, Japan, countries in the Caribbean, and Spanish-speaking and Buddhist countries. However, as was expected, most of the men were from the United States, a few from the northeast, e.g., New York, Philadelphia, but the majority, it seems were from the South. They seemed to be from various socio-economic backgrounds and were White, Latino, Jewish, Japanese, African American, and other ethnicities. A couple were from Buddhist countries (but did not say they were Buddhist), a few were Muslim, but most seemed to be of the Christian faith (or at least that was the faith of their families of origin).

Although a few of the men seem to have had unstable and tragic beginnings, and lived by the "law of the land" and "code of the streets," the majority of them seems to have come from loving, God-fearing and hard-working families with strong family bonds, who also stressed these values, along with values of honesty, respect, independence, etc. when they were growing up; and were taught to get an education so that they not just "survive," but "thrive."

Some of the men spoke of coming from strong-willed families and particularly of "loving" dads, who provided for their entire families, and loving mothers and grandmothers who loved them unconditionally. They spoke of their origins from the "love," "desires," "hopes," and "dreams" of their mothers and fathers and from "the Mother Goddess and the Father, God." They indicated that they are the descendants of peoples from great civilizations; the ancient Mayans, Aztecs, Native Americans, enslaved African Americans (who are the descendants of great African civilizations), and the Gullah Geechee who are also the descendants of African peoples (the Asante, Adjo, Bantu, Fulani, Fon, Hausa, Mandinka, Yoruba, etc.).

The men expressed their appreciation for their humble beginnings when life was simple; when they hunted and fished, communed with and listened to the sounds of nature (some had a deep love and appreciation for nature), played games, looked forward to and played sports; went to church and prayed with their families, listened to country, rock n roll, soul and other types of music; had cook-outs, country boils, barbecues, family reunions, and just simply shared time eating their favorite or national dishes with their families.

A couple of the men described their accomplishments before and after their incarceration, one achieving his GED at the age of 70, and another one achieving his GED at 46, graduating with honors, and being named valedictorian after being diagnosed with brain damage. This man also went from having difficulty "with verbal self-expression," to discovering ways to express himself through writing. A few of the men expressed Black consciousness—that is an awareness of the politics of being a Black man in U.S. society.

Many of the men seem to have a good outlook, do not blame anyone (other than themselves) for their circumstances, and seem to have a lot of hope for the future. Some of the men expressed not holding on to the past, particularly because there is nothing you can do about it and look forward to the future. Some dream that one day they will be free and be able to return to their families. Although they were incarcerated, some of the men expressed their love for America. Most importantly, many of the men seem deeply spiritual and expressed reverence for God or "The Most High."

The voices of the men in *I Am From* are truly inspiring. The hope is that their voices will inspire and empower other men who are in similar circumstances with their insights, hopes, dreams and aspirations and that they might be moved to use their voices to empower and inspire others. It was truly an honor, and a privilege to co-edit with David Martin, *I am From: Voices From a Prison in the South.*

Dr. Ra Heter
(aka Patricia Dixon)

I Am From

I am from America's most populated city that's known to have insomnia.

I am from genealogy whose exact origin is extremely difficult to trace definitively.

I am from the generation known for its "Childbirth boom" (Baby Boomers 1945-1964).

I am from a family who believes that our mission in life is not to merely survive but to strive.

I am from a father who was raised having to fish, hunt, and farm for groceries.

I am from Mason Jar delicacies concocted from recipes known to warm New England's coldest winters.

I am from a dozen U.S. Presidents. Among them were two soldiers, seven sailors, and three non-servicemen that include the first who looks like me.

I am from the U.S. Air Force, the agency responsible for me creating the alias "The Jet Doctor".

I am from the era of Jim Crow to Black Lives Matter.

I Am From

I am from a quadruple of male-only siblings who all married and sired the exact amount of offspring.

I am from a widowed grandmother who had the courage to leave all she ever knew for a place she had never seen AND had the will to become more than the South said she had the RIGHT to be.

I am from a culture where three primary identifiers define my nationality (race). First, I was "colored," then "black," now in the current era, I'm African American.

I am from a country where the military and the monetary have a history of acting like mercenaries by turning parts of this planet into cemeteries.

I am from the United States of America, the self-proclaimed "home of the brave, land of the free!"

David Martin

I Am From

I am from Black magic.

I am from a grandmother who warned "Money don't grow on trees" as she handed me two quarters to buy ice-cream.

I am from the city of the O-Jays, of Sister Sledge, of McFadden & Whitehead, of Gamble and Huff, of the cheesesteak.

I am from where children played Hide & Go Seek, Catch a girl-Kiss a girl, Greenlight go, and where Mr. Softy promised relief from the heat.

I am from Morris, Diamond, Marvine, Oxford, and Broad streets.

I am from a family where the name Jesus reigns supreme.

I am from the sacrifices of a million slaves.

I am from where black lives still don't matter.

I am from a father who never knew me and a mother whose love still amazes me.

I am from the African diaspora.

I am from Black magic.

Hugo Lacasidon

I Am From

I am from a strong-willed woman who loves her family unconditionally.

I am from a strong family who worked hard for everything they have.

I am from a family I'm proud to be a part of

I am from a place with warm days and cool nights.

I am from the sunshine state. I'm a Florida Gator. Go Gators!

Walter Green

I Am From

I am from the testicles of one whom this world calls a "dead-beat" brother.

I am from the womb and will go to the tomb, son, of a murderess mother... (only in self-defense).

I am from her dysfunction and pain to which I place no blame or I stake no claim.

I am from her praying to God and her praising His name in time prayers were answered and blessings came.

I am from a place of poverty born with the name "Royalty."

I am from where Jesus is head of my life and deserves all of my loyalty.

I am from where love has no boundaries even when hate surrounded me God's will found me.

I am from where girls grew up fast and Lil boys died young, where crack destroyed the dreams of mothers and fathers and killed heroes unsung.

I am from "yes sir", "no mam", "thank you" and "please?" Food stamps, the W.I.C. program, and welfare cheese.

I Am From

I am from where it's all done and received with a smile, the humbleness of children and the heart of a child.

I am from where they live by the law of the land and die by the codes of the street.

I am from where if mom and dad didn't work or hustle then their kids didn't eat.

I am from a place that no longer exists and will be forever missed...my first day of school, the first girl I kissed.

I am from faded memories, broken promises where ghosts and spirits of the ones I lost now roam.

I am from over there off of Bankhead, from Bowen Homes where days were seldom peaceful and the nights were violently calm. You may not know who I am but now you know where I AM FROM.

Prince Alexander

I Am From

I am from everywhere and nowhere specific.

I am from an idea.

I am from hope.

I am from passion.

I am from desire.

I am from him.

I am from her.

I am from a dream.

I am from an old Empire.

I am from the Mother Goddess and the Father God.

I am from a town that knows how to cook the greatest tacos.

I am from the unbreakable bond and love from my dad, mom, brothers, and sisters.

I am from where we speak Spanish.

Ernesto Sanchez

I Am From

I am from the crack era which allowed many of our mothers to get hooked on drugs.

I am from where dudes hear gunshots and argue about the type of firearm that was used.

I am from the side of town that employs the local police department.

I am from where cops have quotas and so does planned parenthood.

I am from a target market.

I am from where being exceptional doesn't get you into Harvard or Yale.

I am from where you have to be exceptional in order to stay out of jail.

I am from where it's easier to get a gun than it is to get a job.

I am from gentrification and desperation, so where I'm from it's easy to get robbed.

I am from where mental illness has a familiar name.... we call it "bugged out."

I Am From

I am from where there is an abandoned house next to an abandoned house that's next to an abandoned and another abandoned house.

I am from a place where I don't expect you to understand because where I'm from is easily misunderstood.

I am from a nation with a caste system and I'm from the bottom caste of society.

I am from the hood.

Raynard Humphrey

I Am From

I am from the Creator who created all creation form, built and born enabled to withstand any type of storm.

I am from a family that loves hard and work just as hard, a culture that lived through ancient times that will never be forgotten.

I am from a musical background with the bass and drums. Poetry recited songs.

I am from a place where you had to get it out of the mud when it burned deep like a diamond.

I am from the streets where I went to school and was taught how to be an entrepreneur and innovator.

I am from a Christianity God-fearing mind state, blessed with the potential to be someone great.

I am from down south where news travels fast. I prepare myself for the future because I can't change the past.

Nathan Milner

I Am From

I am from the North where there are four seasons, summer, fall, winter, and spring.

I am from the suburbs and middle-class America.

I am from a blue-collar family where work was a measure of success.

I am from a Catholic upbringing where the services are a lot more reserved and quieter, a vast difference from the South.

I am from a family where education was important and highly regarded.

I am from meat and potato meals that ruled most meals, but all other types of meals were very welcome.

I am from a childhood of sports where the concept of teamwork was learned.

I Am From

I am from a place where holidays were celebrated with friends and family ad food was always present.

I am from a family that supports one another, no matter the circumstance. I would never want to change anything about who or what I am because it has made me who I am today.

Joe Scoppettuolo

I Am From

I am from southern traditions.

I am from good food and family reunions.

I am from working hard but playing even harder.

I am from the Methodist church.

I am from doing to others as I would have them do to me.

I am from slow-moving rivers and aluminum boats.

I am from bluegills biting in the cypress stumps.

I am from sipping bourbon while the full moon rises.

I am from sitting by the campfire and hearing the owls hoot.

I am from Saturday morning deer hunts.

I am from watching a Tom turkey strut.

I am from fish fry's and low county boils.

I am from close friends and enjoying the fruit of tales.

I am from college football on Saturday afternoon.

I Am From

I am from Georgia Southern University-Go Eagles!

I am from God's country, our country, the greatest on earth.

I am from the United States of America.

I am from the mindset, "we cannot change" the past, only the future.

I am from the now and never forgetting what molded us into who we are.

I am from . . . the heart.

William Roberts

I Am From

I am from a place where we eat a lot of corn.

I am from where tortillas and tamales are the norms.

I am from where ancient civilizations left big pyramids like the Mayas and Aztecs once ruined.

I am from where the Spaniards once conquered, and we adopted their language the same.

I am from where a family can be of four brothers, three sisters, and your parents all live in the same home.

I am from where on a birthday fiesta we Mariachis have music playing and kids and adults break the pinata.

I am from where the Virgin Mary has her home.

I am from where the most prominent religion is Catholic.

I am from where it's almost always warm and where I wish I was home.

Jose Gonzalez Trejo

I Am From

I am from a small town in Georgia where everybody knows everybody.

I am from a place that enjoys soul food cooking.

I am from a loving family.

I am from a family that believes in do unto others as you want to be treated.

I am from those who believe that family sticks together no matter how hard times may get.

I am from a strong-willed background.

I am from a place that honors the importance of family values.

Robert Johnson

I Am From

I am from a plantation of rice and farming.

I am from the land that grows mangoes and coconuts.

I am from a community of communism and hatred.

I am from a Khmer speaking language of Cambodia.

I am from a place where people sell merchandise in outdoor markets.

I am from a small family: due to the rule of communism and genocide.

I am from the Land of Buddhism, but I am not one.

I am from a land of spiritual darkness and haunted houses.

I am from a strange land where war destroys schools and teachers are killed.

I Am From

I am from where luxuries of living are rare.

I am from the poorest of the poor.

I am from hot days and cool nights.

Panna Ross

I Am From

I am from Barbados, the island in the sun, where bright white blinding sand line seashores.

I am from the coconut climbing parish called St. Michael, grew up in cave Hill, surrounded by nothing but caves and hills, roaming the cullies and alleyways.

I am from the land where cuckoo and flying fish is our national dish, so tasty, so yummy, oh man! What about the breadfruit, white, and sweet yams, would you like to try some? I know you'll like it if you do.

I am from carnival, bacchanal, crop-over jumping, music-loving Barbados; O my sweet Barbados. I love you and miss you so much! When will I be home again?

I am from America; this is my home too. Crazy as it may be America is where I died, was reborn, and learned to fly spiritually. America has opened my eyes and made me who I am today. Thank you with sincere gratitude!

I am from confusion and madness, or so it may seem, but is this who I am, or what I am supposed to be? I think not, I'm too good for that.

I Am From

I am from the loving caring heart of my beloved great grandmamma, whom I love and miss so much; O grandmammas, your love still lives on within my heart today. Thanks for everything you gave me; you gave me love, and for that l am grateful, thank you!

I am from my beloved mother earth.

I am from "love" and that's who I am!

Derrick Herbert

I Am From

I am from Tokyo-JAPAN

I am from the people who eat Oriental-food
(Rice, fish, vegetables).

I am from a culture that is based on Buddhism.

I am from a religion that is mixed with
Buddhism, Shintoism, and Catholic. I choose
Mennonite.

I am from my parents who've already committed
suicide. (To commit suicide is a part of Japanese
culture).

I am from the people who speak the Japanese-
language.

I am from a group of runners who run a
Marathon-Race.

I am from a city that has four seasons (Spring,
Summer, Autumn, Winter).

Tokimasa Ohgo

I Am From

I am from God's country.

I am from southern hospitality and howdy ya'll.

I am from Georgia flat land.

I am from a strong-willed background where everybody works for everything they have.

I am from a family I am proud to be called a part of me.

I am from hard work and saving.

I am from a family that laughs hard and works even harder.

Kenneth Roberts

I Am From

I am from where nowhere begins and perfection
is out of reach, but I keep reaching.

I am from narrow roads and open minds, eternal
spirits, and better times.

I am from the harmonic sounds of lost souls in
the twilight, searching for equality. Where
"NEVER" doesn't exist, and "CAN'T" doesn't
enter the mind.

I am from A to Z and every sacred letter in
between is still my dream, America.

I am from yesterday's values and today's
technology, Martin's dream, Malcolm's
revolution, Gwendolyn's pen, and the poetic
silence of Langston.

I am from the struggle for justice, lost tears, and
long goodbyes.

I am from the dust that blows on country roads,
where creeks and fields of nature's gold stand by
for you to behold.

I am from in between the truth and reality, where
nowhere begins.

Mr. Prentiss Gardley

I Am From

I am from our higher power.

I am from two very loving parents who are worthy of all the blessings God showers upon them.

I am from a state that we call "God's country"!

I am from a place where people don't hate on each other, instead, they lift one another up as if they are family.

I am from a place where an extra dinner plate is set for unexpected company.

I am from a place where you can see the leaves full of color in the fall as if the hills were ablaze.

I am from a place where you can hear the bullfrog's "ribbit" at night.

I am from a place where Mormons and Quakers live.

I am from the great state of Ohio.

James Nicholas

I Am From

I am from a family where the people are gregarious and outgoing, but I was an outcast who stuttered and suffered from an undiagnosed mental illness.

I am from my only human friend, who during my teenaged years, was a developmentally challenged uncle. I had to sign the documents to remove him from life support after he suffered a heart attack later in our lives.

I am from going mute for a time at age 14, after witnessing my cousin get run over by a car, but no one noticed because of my intentional alienation from everyone, but my uncle.

I am from finding peace and solace in the solitude of the outdoors.

I am from bubbling creeks whispering to me in the still of the night.

I am from those same creeks going dry and silent in the heat of summer.

I am from being friends with a dog that shared its secret places with me.

I Am From

I am from quitting school in the 6th grade to becoming self-educated.

I am from brain damage at 32 to getting my GED at 46, graduating with honors, and being named valedictorian.

I am from having a difficult time with verbal self-expression to discovering a way to do so through writing.

Ricky Edwards

I Am From

I am from Atlanta where everybody can get creative in their own ways.

I am from a neighborhood where we grew up in poverty and learned never to be foolish but to gain understanding and wisdom.

I am from a city where corrupt officers, lawyers, prosecutors, and judges arrest, harm and kill innocent people without reason.

I am from a family where their love is strong, and we pray through the hardest of times.

I am from a town where every black man hopes for brighter days.

I am from where people kick you when you're down, but when you're doing better than before everyone wants to be your friend.

I am from a place where authority is oppressive, and we are labeled as something which we are not.

I am from the birthplace of a civil rights icon, Dr. Martin Luther King Jr., who said regardless of our skin color we must join together in harmony as brothers and sisters. Unfortunately, it appears

I Am From

as if we oppress our own kind instead of lifting one another up.

I am from a place where everyone prays for the thanksgiving received from the Lord and thank Him for everything that He does for us.

I am from a place where things happen for a purpose because God's place is much better than our understanding and knowledge.

I am from a city where times get hard and make you want to quit but by having faith in the Lord combined with courage, we never give up.

I am from a place where we know that by keeping God first, we can overcome anything.

Charles Stewart

I Am From

I am from a place where people don't understand.

I am from a thought that people think otherwise.

I am from a being that can't be described.

I am from a place that you can only be guided to from the Al -Khaliq (creator).

I am from a time that has already been decided.

I am from a great man who has already taught me wisdom and how to have great character.

I am from a place that I've yet had the opportunity to visit.

I am from a place where if you are not right the hooks on the bridge of Sirat will snatch you into Jahannam (hell).

I am from a place that helps me become a better person.

I am from a congealed clot.

I am from where I can recognize that Allah exists by looking at the sun, moon, stars and natural disasters.

I Am From

I am from the one who created the heavens and hells!

I am from the one who will end the life that I am living.

I am from the Deen of Al-Islam which Allah has chosen and perfected for me: I am Muslim.

Marcus Wilson aka Tari!

I Am From

I am from the divine purpose of bringing glory to God.

I am from a rare breed of men who resists compromising integrity.

I am from a demonstration of raw power in the spiritual as well as in the flesh.

I am from being reserved from a world that is to serve God in the world to come anew.

I am from among the ones that are labeled "the meek."

I am from a leader of a righteous path I have chosen.

I am from patience for the sake of time that waits for no man.

I am from loyalty for my own sake because others must learn loyalty from someone else.

I am from my own world in my own realm viewing everyone's life through a pair of brown eyes.

I am from love because I respect it.

I Am From

I am from respect because I love my culture.

I am from Louisiana, a state that's true to its southern hospitality.

I am from Me, Myself, and I!

Cortez Carter

I Am From

I am from being born male by nature but becoming a man by choice.

I am from being a man by principle; I live not just because of the deepness of my voice.

I am from my mother's son, a brother, cousin, nephew, and to many...a friend.

I am from a protector of a woman, like when Adam and Eve began.

I am from a compilation of knowledge that I constantly try to apply; a living soul embodied with a spirit that will never die.

I am from being bold enough to stand up for my beliefs even in the midst of strife.

I am from being a man who will sacrifice his own life for certain things.

I am from being a man who looks beyond what I can see with the naked eye.

I am from being a man who recognizes deception when Satan tries to lie.

I Am From

I am from being a man that recognizes that struggle can make you stronger.

I am from being a man who realizes that in today's society what's right is often viewed as wrong.

I am from becoming a man who knows I can triumph regardless of my past life.

I am from becoming a man who believes in my heart that I can do all things through Christ.

Carlos Koonce

I Am From

I am from northwest Georgia.

I am from the foothills of the Blue Ridge mountains, land often referred to as that of the Hillbilly.

I am from Dalton, Georgia; the self-proclaimed "world's carpet capital."

I am from parents who built with their own two hands, the house that my aging mother still resides in.

I am from blond hair and blue eyes.

I am from a great grandmother who, from an ancient photograph, it's obvious to determine, came from an indigenous North American tribe I've never known.

I am from the nationality called Caucasian.

I am from the Caucasus Mountains of Asia.

I am from a family of Christians, but I've chosen the Jehovah's Witness following.

Tom Scroggins

I Am From

I am from the deep south where people still say "please" and "thank you."

I am from great tasting southern cuisine.

I am from a chaotic period in this country's history, the fifties, sixties, and seventies.

I am from English speaking parents.

I am from a mother who never knew hers.

I am from a family of five siblings where I am the most senior.

I am from a Christian faith but choose Baptist beliefs.

I am from whatever I choose to be.

Jerry Thompson

I Am From

I am from an open mind.

I am from a free spirit.

I am from broken English, proper English, and heart to heart communication.

I am from where we value where we are going more than where we are from.

I am from where everybody is family and everybody means everything.

I am from interstate 85 North, North Indian Trail and Quick Trip.

I am from throw-em-up, bust-em-up, and nigga knockin'.

I am from jollof rice and cassava leaf.

I am from parents who didn't know their birth dates but celebrated ours.

I am from where life is short and Jesus never fails.

Sehweh Willie

I Am From

I am from one of America's poorest societies, the coal miners of eastern Kentucky.

I am from a Christian culture where Jesus lives in all of his children.

I am from America where ALL LIVES should matter.

I am from "Dawg Country," home of the University of Georgia.

I am from parents where all we had to eat were beans and rice every day during a recession in 1958.

I am from the culture that when necessary I would work every day for a month instead of expecting a handout.

I am from a culture where I believe that someday I and many of my acquainted offenders will once again be free.

Thomas McKendrick

I Am From

I am from an era when little children played
"Ring Around the Rosey."

I am from a Swedish community.

I am from where addresses are rural routes as
opposed to street names.

I am from where the state's soil is my hometown's
name.

I am from the state where Kool-Aid was invented.

I am from where stalks of corn outnumber
people.

I am from where country roads outnumber
highways.

I am from a place where the corn grows as
straight as an arrow.

I am from where the color of money starts off as
"yellow."

I am from a city named after an Indian tribe.

I am from where everyone says it's the good life.

I Am From

I am from a state where you can drive to high school at age fourteen.

I am from a state that has a museum called "Pioneer Village."

I am from a multi-cultural family. German, Panamanian, African American, and Mexican.

I am from a city where you can get a "Runza" to eat.

I am from a city where I was the only African American child.

I am from a place I pray to return to one day.

Thomas Schwartz

I Am From

I am from a broken home.

I am from a family full of love shared among one another.

I am from a generation of strong-willed ancestors.

I am from German, Irish, and Cherokee descendants.

I am from the Creator, the Most High God.

I am from the One that provides strength, grace and a future.

I am from God fearing people.

I am from a place where we stick together through fair weather days and stormy nights.

I am from a place where we have to put in the work, day after day for the greater good.

I am from the same place as you, it only appears different because of the paths we've taken in our lives.

Tim Highland

I Am From

I am from a country that will always welcome you with open arms.

I am from a country that has much diversity.

I am from a country where your word is your best contract.

I am from a place where vacation spots are plentiful.

I am from a country where you will find a wide variety of regional fruits.

I am from "South of the Border"...MEXICO!

Miguel Martinez

I Am From

I am from an era where children were giving birth to children.

I am from a mother whose age precedes mine by thirteen years.

I am from a mother who, by age twenty-five, had five children.

I am from several states, conceived in Georgia, and born in the back seat of a taxi during a heavy Maryland snowstorm.

I am from MD, VA, NC, SC and GA.

I am from lots of crying and tears. Mom cried often as she tried to explain why we had to move constantly and change schools frequently.

I am from "hand-me-downs" and full of gratitude for the numerous churches and folk who shared their benefactions during holidays.... especially Christmas, "yes"!

I am from a dinner table that consisted of Vienna Sausage, potted meat, bologna, and if lucky.... fried Spam!

I Am From

I am from a mom who gave her entire teenage years, young adulthood, and adulthood to her children.

I am from being able to say, "thank you mom for staying with us and not giving up"!

James Owens

I Am From

I am from God who is my Author and Father.

I am from middle Georgia, also known as the "heart of the state."

I am from a loving mother AND a loving father.

I am from a family that believes that hard work pays off.

I am from Peace.

I am from Love.

I am from the dirt roads.

I am from a place that I am ready to return to.

Alphonia Leary

I Am From

I am from the home of the Virgin of Guadalupe.

I am from a place where we cultivate.

I am from where the most prominent religion is Catholicism.

I am from a town known to cook the greatest tacos and burritos.

I am from where we speak Spanish.

I am from the ancient civilizations of the Maya, Aztecs, and Toltecs.

I am from Tabasco state in SE Mexico on the Caribbean Southwest of the Yucatán Peninsula, whose capital is Villahermosa.

I am from where my people rise early every day to work in the fields.

Regulo Braco Lopez

I Am From

I am from a church-going, God fearing family.

I am from a place where respect is shown by saying "yes sir" and "yes ma'am."

I am from an upbringing of love, respect, honesty, and discipline.

I am from out in the country (the "sticks") where deer frequently jump out in front of your car as you drive.

I am from a broken home but still taught chivalry...holding doors open for ladies and pulling out their chairs before sitting.

I am from a place with plenty of land, raised on 27 acres to hunt, fish, and ride four-wheelers and dirt bikes.

I am from a place where Walmart is approximately a twenty-minute drive, and we hear crickets and whip-poor-wills at night.

I am from a family where you get to have dessert after you finish your meal.

I Am From

I am from a family that raises horses and cows on our farm. We have our own rodeo and rope our own cattle.

I am from a place where in the summer you can leap off a rope swing into the Savannah River.

I am from a family of the oldest lineage where our Creator sent our Savior to die and save us from sin.

Zachary Hyman

I Am From

I am from a family that worships and believes in the Most High.

I am from a strong, supportive family.

I am from a hard-working, never give up, educated loving dad, who's a "go-getter."

I am from a hard-working, strong and courageous mom who is very loving.

I am from a household with two strong Black parents.

I am from a family that believes in doing better by making the best out of your life.

I am from a small country town that I pray will grow into a more successful place.

I am from a household that loves to cook.

I am from all of the previously mentioned things but most of all I'm from a trusting, faithful, and awesome Creator.

Christian M. Brinson

I Am From

I am from West Virginia.

I am from the Baby Boomer era, (b.1958).

I am from a family that believes in God.

I am from a hard-working family.

I am from a family of thirteen siblings to which I was born first.

I am from a United States Military family.

I am from a strong-willed father.

I am from a family that loves to fish and hunt.

I am from the Church of God.

Charles E. Nobles

I Am From

I am from a loving, kind and gentle family that have good morals and respect for each other.

I am from a mother who believed in the old-fashioned Christian life.

I am from a father who believes in the philosophy "an eye for an eye and a tooth for a tooth."

I am from a grandmother who'd backhand you if you spoke when not spoken to.

I am from a country where its citizens are all brave.

I am from a country that states that its citizens are FREE, but I know that's not true.

I am from a state where we have the freedom of speech but now, I'm in a place where I no longer have that freedom.

I am from living in a world that I am truly not from, the sooner I can return to my rightful mind, body, and soul then I will be who I truly am, the person God made me to be.

Bobby Pitts

I Am From

I am from one of the thirteen original colonies.

I am from a state known for corn and steel piers.

I am from a mother who birthed eight and a father that provided for all of us.

I am from seven older siblings who helped raise me.

I am from a family that celebrated birthdays together.

I am from the lessons that I was taught.

I am from the freedom my parents allowed me to have and the morals that they instilled in me.

I am from the mistakes I've made and from the darkness of depression.

I am from all of this and more, but really, I am from where the Lord wants me to be so I can experience things from where I am today.

Steven Pease

I Am From

I am from the womb of my mother and the testis of my father.

I am from coastal Georgia, the Savannah region.

I am from low country boils, crab rice, smothered fish, shrimp and grits.

I am from where Savannahian's say ... "over they" instead of "over there."

I am from where the Port of Savannah saw millions of slaves arrive on ships then beaten and sold off like animals.

I am from where everyone visits the "root doctor" when they get in trouble, but not yours truly.

I am from the wicked streets of Savannah where they'll spank you if you disrespect them.

I am from block parties, cookouts, house parties, spade games and big ass dice games.

I am from love and loyalty.

I am from a city where everything is turned GREEN during St. Patrick's Day, including the river.

I Am From

I am from a black community where the government declared war on drugs when they were actually turning a blind eye from the real truth.

I am from ancient history.

I am from a world that's filled with both hate and love.

I am from the thoughts of God...so where are YOU from?

Edward T. Chisholm

I Am From

I am from the "country."

I am from a God-fearing family.

I am from where we work hard and drink moonshine even harder.

I am from a lakefront town.

I am from the best Hartwell Dam.

I am from where the high school mascot is a bulldog.

I am from the backwoods.

I am from a place where people help one another regardless of color.

Dwayne Craft

I Am From

I am from Christian parents.

I am from a small town in north Georgia, the self-proclaimed "carpet capital of the world."

I am from the bad streets of Chicago.

I am from "semper fidelis"......the United States Marine Corp.

I am from the jungles of Vietnam where I never wanted to kill anyone. I only wanted to prevent someone from killing me.

I am from a "brotherhood" where a "brother" would give his life for another.

I am from a Faith and Character Based community where we think, speak, act, and strive with what we have to be our best.

Jimmy Greeson

I Am From

I am from a place that has four seasons that include blistery HOT summers and "blizzardly" cold winters.

I am from the home of "Dorothy and Toto," who traveled to the land of "OZ."

I am from the gospel and the blues.

I am from Friday night football and barbecues.

I am from attending church every Sunday morning.

I am from a family that prays together and loves one another.

I am from a place where children chase lightning bugs at night while parents and neighbors relax on the porch.

I am from the poor side of the tracks although I never felt its poverty.

I am from a place where bullets try to find a home within you.

I am from a place where violence breeds more violence.

I Am From

I am from a place where your own friends and family try to pull you down.

I am from a place where the system is broken, and it's designed for me to fail.

I am from a place that gives you hope, but if you're not careful, it will sidetrack you with prison, negativity, and DOPE.

I am from a place where your word means everything.

I am from a place that, should you choose to do so, you can rise up and determine your destiny!

Frank Selkirk

I Am From

I am from the Middle East.

I am from a country where it's capital is the most important city in religious history.

I am from a country where military service is mandatory.

I am from Judaism, an Israeli from Tel-Aviv, the grandchild of a holocaust survivor.

I am from a country where public transportation is the most widely used method of travel.

I am from where olive trees are a symbol of strength and beauty.

I am from a culture that loves soccer.

I am from a country where the primary diet consists of fish and vegetables.

I am from a land that houses Jews from many nations.

I am from a casualty of the Justice System.

I Am From

I am from a beautiful country, a country the bible says is to be our birthright.

I am from where flowers bloom even in the desert.

I am from a family with European and Eurasian roots.

I am from a country where the youth guard its borders.

I am from a dream realized in 1948.

Dean Arce

I Am From

I am from America the country that is called the "melting pot" due to its great diversity of cultures.

I am from a genealogy that has yet to be traced.

I am from the "Muscle Car" generation and the birth of musical diversity like rock, gospel, funk, soul, new age and country.

I am from a family that was like a pack of dogs.

I am from a father who was a career U.S Marine who had no idea how to be a father.

I am from a teen mother who left her children with my father at age 17 and then ran off with another man.

I am from being raised by my father's sister who dropped out of Nun College in order to care for both me and her mother.

I am from a home where we relocated every couple of years.

I Am From

I am from the middle class and the poor white classes of people.

I am from where not one, but ALL of your actions define you.

James Jones

I Am From

I am from a military family where rules, duties, obligations, and freedoms were clearly established and strictly enforced.

I am from a form of life where hard work, independence, being frugal, self-reliant and content were highly valued.

I am from a sportsman's past with the ability to survive and prosper within meager means; killed by surviving with nature through hunting, fishing, and foraging for food.

I am from a very diverse past of world travel, life experiences, and trauma ... the events of life.

I am from where there is a monument in the city of an insect...a boll weevil.

Gary Blalock

I Am From

I am from a loving, caring family from Macon, Georgia.

I am from God who's the reason that I am here.

I am from a place that enjoys soul food.

I am from a family that believes in doing unto others as you'd have others do unto you.

I am from HOPE.

I am from Passion.

I am from Him.

I am from Her.

I am from a Dream.

Ardis Hunter

I Am From

I am from happily married parents who raised nine sons.

I am from a mother who birthed me as her middle child on the same month and day of her own birth.

I am from the term "Grady Baby" which recognizes a prestigious hospital in Georgia's capital city.

I am from a God-fearing family that raised their children in the church, resulting in several familial pastors and ministers.

I am from the "Dirty South," the "Peach State."

I am from the home of the nationally known historic Black church called Ebenezer Baptist; also, the home of the Historical Black College and University known as the Atlanta University (AU) Center.

Angelo Starks

I Am From

I am from a father, a son, and a brother.

I am from a city that taught me to give back to my community.

I am from a family of firefighters and first responders and am one myself.

I am from being a trucker to becoming a family provider.

I am from believing in God.

I am from a man of a few words.

Chris Critcher

I Am From

I am from the smallest conterminous country in the Americas and the only one without a Caribbean coastline.

I am from the indigenous civilizations of the Maya, Pipil and Lenca peoples who faced a long struggle with Spain during its quest to take away our land upon their arrival in 1524.

I am from where the most prominent religion is Catholicism and Jesus is the country's savior.

I am from a place where we love to eat Pupusas, the country's national food.

I am from the 1980s when during a 12-year civil war some 70,000 people died, (thousands more "disappeared"), and we continue to struggle from the hardships of its lingering effects.

I am from a land where our favorite sport is FUTBOL!

I am from Costa del Sol (Sun Coast) where people rise early to catch fish for both sustenance and prosperity.

I Am From

I am from tropical temperatures that range between 80-90 degrees Fahrenheit and we experience two seasons...summer and the rainy season.

I am from where English is our second language and Spanish is official.

I am from El Salvador..."viva"!

William Bernal Cortez

I Am From

I am from a home with six siblings full of love.

I am from a city within a city, Vine City is its name.

I am from the best food ever cooked on a wood-burning stove.

I am from seeing white-robed men wearing hoods on their heads walk the streets.

I am from Black communities fighting against oppression.

I am from where "united we stand" lived up to its meaning.

I am from breaking away from family traditions to pursuing my own dreams.

I am from becoming a teenaged father to currently being a great grandfather.

I am from getting my G.E.D at the age of seventy.

I am from working a shoeshine booth to walking on a modeling runway.

I am from dropping out of high school to starting my own company.

I Am From

I am from "back of the bus" laws to pursuing Small Businessman of the Year.

I am from a child of God and God's unique creation.

Eugene Neal

I Am From

I am from a historical black community, (HBC), consisting of a family built in 1940 that is filled with love, joy, values, and twelve gauges.

I am from a community filled with black-owned property, homes, and businesses.

I am from a community of black men that mastered the science of breaking in wild horses on a small farm up the road.

I am from a community of families that, during a storm when power is lost, everyone fires up their grills and fellowships together.

I am from an "HBC" consisting of two black-owned churches and a three-level ministry that feeds the hungry.

I am from an "HBC" where all residents before and after desegregation, faithfully sent the children to the same historic school in our neighborhood.

I Am From

I am from an "HBC" where the streets in every compass direction are named after the late principal of our community's historic school.

I am from a historic black community of family and black cowboys...."breathe black man, breathe"!

Mr. Gary King

I Am From

I am from the merger of a king and queen who instilled within me the goal of greatness.

I am from a family of boys whose number equals that of the girls...three.

I am from where right is not always "right" because quite often your "rights" are violated by a system of injustice and corruption.

I am from the mindset of self-preservation and self-awareness and where survival is one's only mission in life.

I am from a loving family whose happiness means the world to me.

LaMario Echols

I Am From

I am from Rincon Georgia.

I am from a family that made its own way by starting their own business.

I am from a family that puts a lot of stock in sports and motorcycle racing.

I am from a family with high values and ideals which I try very hard to uphold.

Michael Murdock

I Am From

I am from a place that is found now only in my mind.

I am from some places I can no longer find.

I am from the "country", where things were a lot simpler than now.

I am from sneaking across pastures to fish and being chased by the cows.

I am from a home where God was no stranger.

I am from a time when we had little but was always willing to share.

I am from a time when at night we slept and left the doors wide open.

I am from my grandparent's home, a place where I always felt warm and safe.

I am from a place where our neighbors were always welcome.

I am from parents who had to scrape but did so with pride.

I am from a place where whip-poor-wills sang me to sleep outside my window each night.

I Am From

I am from grandparents who tried to teach me
right from wrong.

I am from a time when country, bluegrass, and
rock-n-roll played on our radio.

I am from these memories that will travel with me
everywhere I go.

I am from bright summer days fishing, days I
wished would never end.

I am from a time of sharing my Ne-Hi and
Cracker Jacks with my friend.

I am from fields of hay and praying for a good
breeze.

I am from all of these blessings that I sometimes
forget to give thanks for when I'm down on my
knees.

I am from a time when you fell in love and
matrimony was for a lifetime.

I am from a place where it was OK to mention
the intimate moments that you had with your wife
out in public.

I Am From

I am from a God who blessed me with all of the aforementioned gifts and so much more.

I am from knowing that He blessed us even though we were poor. He was there when I married, and when my daughters came into the world. I witnessed God's miracles when I looked into the eyes of my baby girls.

I am from places that now feel as if they only exist in my dreams. I've been away so long.....an eternity it seems.

I am from knowing it wasn't the raising of my family or even my home as to reasons why I'm here...it's my fault and mine alone.

I am from that other world and that prison will never belong.

I am from faith that one day God will deliver me home.

James Farr

I Am From

I am from a place where peaches are sweet and red clay lay under your feet.

I am from where we love college football..."Go Dawgs!"

I am from the state known for its many shades of color and the smell of soul food in the air.

Christopher Owens

I Am From

I am from Cherokee, North Carolina.

I am from a big family tree.

I am from a good father.

I am from a good mother.

I am from a descendent of the Cherokee tribe.

I am from traditional Native American folklore, dance, and smoking "peace pipes."

I am from this wonderful place called the USA.

Chris Edwards

I Am From

I am from New England and cold winters.

I am from Massachusetts, the Commonwealth state... Boston.

I am from a family of gamblers.

I am from an environment where success doesn't matter.

I am from Allah.

Riley Harrison

I Am From

I am from history that's an unending conversation between the past and the present but can ultimately change the future.

I am from the South and its multitudes...Southern hope, Southern fear, Southern joy, Southern sadness, Southern tragedy, and Southern triumph.

I am from descendants of former enslaved Africans who lived along the Southeastern coasts of South Carolina and Georgia....the "low country," home of treasured Sea Island cotton.

I am from ancient communities that preserve many African traditions and a language dialect that became known as Gullah or Geechee...my way of life.

I am from American history during a time when most people want American mythology.

I am from the endangered traditions of the Gullah Geechee people of Charleston and James Island, South Carolina. Also, of Savannah, Hilton Head, and Daufuskie, Georgia.

I Am From

I am from a generation who thought that being Gullah Geechee carried negative connotations but not for my forefathers. They carried the names with pride.

I am from where the education of my people, and understanding who we are, is missing. It's not the culture that is vanishing but the teaching about my culture, and our history, and our roots that is vanishing.

I am from African descendants who were the first slaves brought here from countries on the Gulf of Guinea.

I am from a mixture of Asante, Adjo, Bantu, Fulani, Fon, Hausa, Mandinka, and Yoruba peoples; just to name a few.

Anonymous

I Am From

I am from a time when the world was transformed by the use of nouns which instantly became household words, such as PANDEMIC, QUARANTINE, SOCIAL DISTANCING, RISING DEATH TOLL, and CORONAVIRUS.

I am from a generation that thrives in the virtual world but was cut off from the physical world because of government forced isolation.

I am from a coterie of survivors who were infected with a virus that is concealed and capable of being discovered but currently has no cure.

I am from the Baby Boomer era when widespread protests and unrest over systemic racism and injustice seem to never cease to make headlines across America. This time around the motto is called "Black Lives Matter"!

I am from a nation led by a president who isn't competent enough to take effective action during a crisis or toward ending the separation of the races but instead acts like a bigot himself.

Anonymous

I Am From

I am from a family that cares and loves unconditionally.

I am from grandparents who worked hard to properly raise four children in a two-bedroom house without running water.

I am from a family that took advantage of every opportunity to give me a "good" life.

I am from a woman who taught school during the seventies and eighties and always taught me to keep my head up and not mistreat anyone.

I am from a family of doctors, lawyers, and politicians who never looked down on others because of their status.

I am from a family of hard-working, law-abiding citizens who worked hard like the masses to make it.

I am from a Georgia native and raised approximately thirty miles from UGA. "Go Dawgs"!

I am from a family who always said, "set your goals high and NEVER give up."

Anonymous

I Am From

I am from:
A union of strangers, where drifting lives range
One with a few bills perhaps even change
The other willing to give her body in exchange.

I am from:
A most fallacious start as can be
A ward of the state my destiny...maybe
But strength lies deep within a "Trick Baby."

I am from:
A rescuing family who compassionately took me in
A new mother, father, and sister were now my kin
They taught me hope, love, and gave me strength
within.

I am from:
A generation of peace and war
Peace is a compromise, so I chose war
So I learned to kill and became worse than
before.

I Am From

I am from:
A deep-rooted issue I needed to overcome
A trait overlooked by many but noticed by some
As I grasped at rungs of straw and ate crumb by
crumb.

I am from:
Ruined relationships yes marriage too
Successes there were but far too few
The blame is on me, but these words are for you.

I am from:
Many persons, places, and things
Doubt not that the caged bird sings
Simply sit in awe and be amazed when he spreads
his wings.

Wayne Krier